THE STAR SPANGLED BANNER

Cristie Reed

Rourke
Educational Media

rourkeeducationalmedia.com

Before Reading:

Building Academic Vocabulary and Background Knowledge

Before reading a book, it is important to tap into what your child or students already know about the topic. This will help them develop their vocabulary, increase their reading comprehension, and make connections across the curriculum.

1. *Look at the cover of the book. What will this book be about?*
2. *What do you already know about the topic?*
3. *Let's study the Table of Contents. What will you learn about in the book's chapters?*
4. *What would you like to learn about this topic? Do you think you might learn about it from this book? Why or why not?*
5. *Use a reading journal to write about your knowledge of this topic. Record what you already know about the topic and what you hope to learn about the topic.*
6. *Read the book.*
7. *In your reading journal, record what you learned about the topic and your response to the book.*
8. *After reading the book complete the activities below.*

Content Area Vocabulary
Read the list. What do these words mean?

anthem
commissioned
interfering
mortar
patriotism
peninsula
prosperous
ransacked
relentless
sloop
troops

After Reading:

Comprehension and Extension Activity

After reading the book, work on the following questions with your child or students in order to check their level of reading comprehension and content mastery.

1. *Where is the national anthem played? (Summarize)*
2. *Which president signed the law making "The Star-Spangled Banner" the national anthem? (Summarize)*
3. *What contributed to the War of 1812? (Asking questions)*
4. *Why is it significant to have "The Star-Spangled Banner" set to the tune of a popular British song? (Infer)*
5. *How should you react when the national anthem is played? (Text to self connection)*

Extension Activity

The poem that was later made into our national anthem was inspired by events of the War of 1812. Create a timeline starting with the events leading up the War of 1812 and ending with the president signing the law making "The Star Spangled Banner" our national anthem. Be sure to have detailed events on your timeline.

TABLE OF CONTENTS

"THE STAR-SPANGLED BANNER"

"The Star-Spangled Banner" became the national **anthem** of the United States of America in 1931. When it was written 117 years before, it was simply a poem about a special flag. That special flag was a symbol of freedom. It represented the bravery and **patriotism** of the citizens of the United States of America.

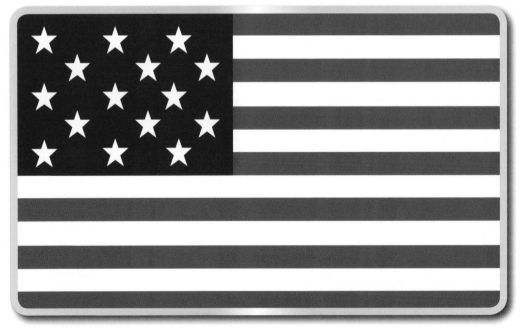

This is what the flag looked like in 1814 when the song was written.

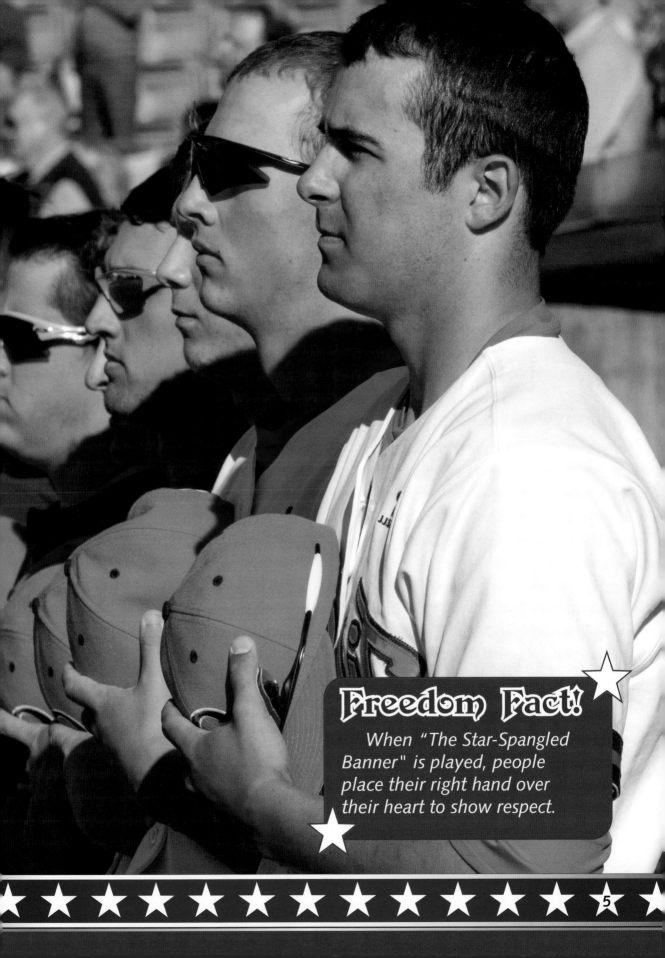

Freedom Fact!

When "The Star-Spangled Banner" is played, people place their right hand over their heart to show respect.

THE WAR OF 1812

When the Revolutionary War ended in 1783, the United States had won its independence from Britain. The young country was becoming **prosperous**. Trade with other countries increased.

America and Britain negotiated the Treaty of Paris, which ended the American Revolutionary War.

France had supported America in its war for independence. So the U.S. and France had a good trade relationship. But in the early 1800s, Britain, who was now at war with France, started **interfering** with French and American trade. British ships would stop American ships and search them. They kidnapped British-born American sailors. The sailors were forced to work for the British Navy.

Because they needed more sailors in their navy, the British attacked American ships and impressed any sailors who had been born in Britain.

Soon, the British began recruiting Native Americans to join in battles against United States soldiers. In June 1812, President James Madison went to Congress and asked them to declare war on Britain.

Battles between the United States and Britain began in 1812. The war continued for more than two years. It was a difficult war for America. Britain had a mighty navy, many warships, and thousands of **troops**.

On August 24, 1814, British troops marched into the capital city of Washington, D.C. They set fire to homes. They burned the Capitol Building and the Treasury Building. They **ransacked** and burned the president's home. After two days destroying the city, the British began to withdraw. They set their sights on Baltimore, Maryland.

James Madison
1751–1836

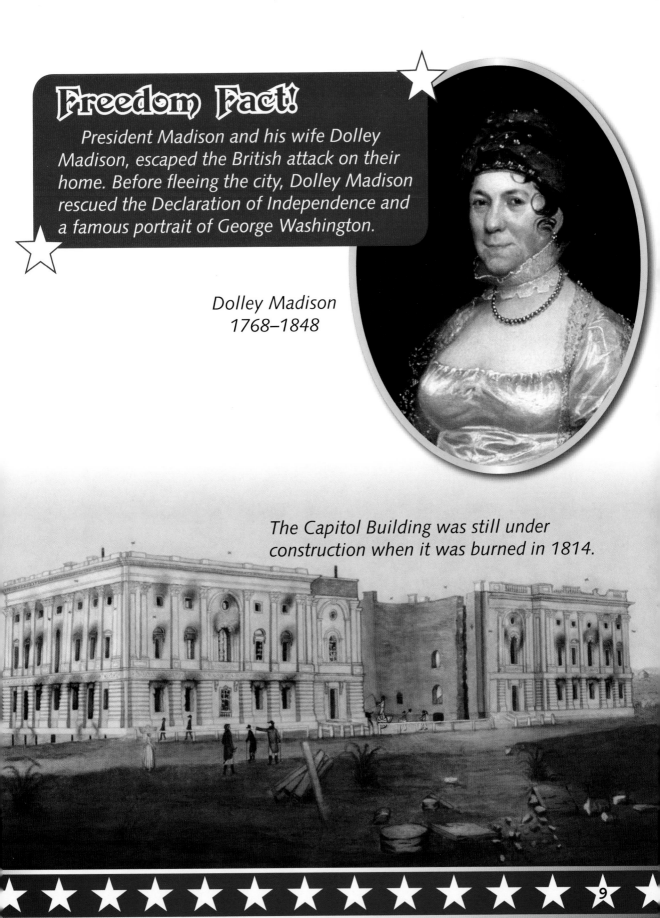

Freedom Fact!

President Madison and his wife Dolley Madison, escaped the British attack on their home. Before fleeing the city, Dolley Madison rescued the Declaration of Independence and a famous portrait of George Washington.

Dolley Madison
1768–1848

The Capitol Building was still under construction when it was burned in 1814.

Baltimore, Maryland is located in the northeastern corner of the Chesapeake Bay. The city had an important shipping port. The British wanted to overtake the city so they could bring their own ships into the harbor. From there, they could bring in supplies and reinforcement troops. The only thing standing in their way was Fort McHenry.

Fort McHenry sat on a **peninsula** just south of Baltimore. British ships could not reach Baltimore unless they could get past the fort. The British planned to attack Fort McHenry from the water.

The Battle of Baltimore

In the Battle of Baltimore, the British fleet sailed up the Patapsco River from Chesapeake Bay.

On September 13, 1814, the British attacked. They bombarded Fort McHenry with bombs and rockets for twenty-five hours. Cannon balls, **mortar** rounds, and Congreve rockets sailed through the air. Their fiery glow was reflected in great clouds of smoke. Explosions echoed off the walls of the fort.

About 1,000 soldiers at Fort McHenry defended the fort against the British fleet.

Congreve Rocket

The British were **relentless** in their attack. At times, more than one rocket per minute sailed through the sky. Intense shelling continued through the day and into the night. Despite the heavy firepower, many of the bombs missed their target. The British decided to close in on Fort McHenry.

U.S. soldiers were ready to attack once the ships came within their range. Cannons and guns fired back. The Americans sank two British warships. The remaining British ships withdrew. The British attack had failed. Baltimore was saved.

Fort McHenry stands today as a monument to the brave defense of Baltimore.

FRANCIS SCOTT KEY

From a British warship several miles away, Francis Scott Key was negotiating for the release of American prisoners, one of whom was his friend, Dr. William Beanes. The British agreed to the prisoners' release. However, by this time the British were deeply involved in the fight for Fort McHenry. They did not want Key to give away any information that could help the American troops. They ordered Key to wait on their ship until the battle was over.

Francis Scott Key
1779–1843

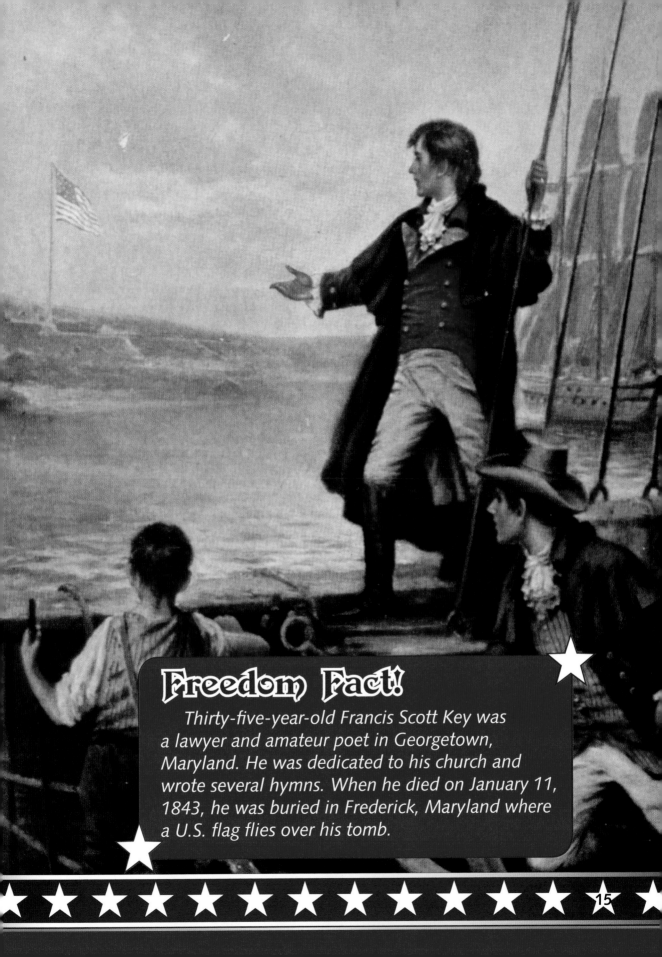

Freedom Fact!

Thirty-five-year-old Francis Scott Key was a lawyer and amateur poet in Georgetown, Maryland. He was dedicated to his church and wrote several hymns. When he died on January 11, 1843, he was buried in Frederick, Maryland where a U.S. flag flies over his tomb.

The men witnessed the fierce battle between the British and the Americans. When the battle ended, they feared the worst. The air was filled with smoke from the shelling. They were unable to see the fort from the ship. On the morning of September 14, they were released. As they sailed their **sloop** toward the fort, the smoke cleared. They saw the enormous U.S. flag. It was still flying over Fort McHenry. The sight of the gleaming stars and bright stripes waving in the breeze meant victory for the United States. The Americans had defeated the most powerful navy in the world.

At that moment, Key felt so inspired that he took a pen and paper from his pocket and composed a poem. He called his poem "The Defense of Fort McHenry." His poem told a story about the battle he witnessed and the flag that remained standing as a symbol of victory.

Freedom Fact!

Francis Scott Key's original draft of "The Defense of Fort McHenry," was handwritten with quill and ink. Key's poem had four stanzas. The document is on display at the Maryland Historical Society in Baltimore.

O say can you see by the dawn's early light
What so proudly we hail'd at the twilight's last gleaming,
Whose broad stripes & bright stars through the perilous fight
O'er the ramparts we watch'd, were so gallantly streaming?
And the rocket's red glare, the bomb bursting in air,
Gave proof through the night that our flag was still there,
O say does that star-spangled banner yet wave
O'er the land of the free & the home of the brave?

On the shore dimly seen through the mists of the deep,
Where the foe's haughty host in dread silence reposes,
What is that which the breeze, o'er the towering steep,
As it fitfully blows, half conceals, half discloses?
Now it catches the gleam of the morning's first beam,
In full glory reflected now shines in the stream,
'Tis the star-spangled banner — O long may it wave
O'er the land of the free & the home of the brave!

And where is that band who so vauntingly swore,
That the havoc of war & the battle's confusion
A home & a Country should leave us no more?
Their blood has wash'd out their foul footstep's pollution.
No refuge could save the hireling & slave
From the terror of flight or the gloom of the grave,
And the star-spangled banner in triumph doth wave
O'er the land of the free & the home of the brave.

O thus be it ever when freemen shall stand
Between their lov'd home & the war's desolation!
Blest with vict'ry & peace may the heav'n rescued land
Praise the power that hath made & preserv'd us a nation!
Then conquer we must, when our cause it is just,
And this be our motto — "In God is our trust,"
And the star-spangled banner in triumph shall wave
O'er the land of the free & the home of the brave.

FORT MCHENRY'S FLAG

Major George Armistead had taken command of Fort McHenry on June 13, 1813, several months before the British attack. He requested a special flag for the fort. He wanted it to be so big that the British could easily see it from a far distance.

Armistead **commissioned** the flag from Mary Young Pickersgill, a skilled Baltimore flag maker. Her daughter and two nieces assisted, doing all the work by hand. This enormous flag measured 42 feet (13 meters) wide and 30 feet (9 meters) high. The flag had 15 stripes and 15 stars. When finished, the flag weighed over 200 pounds (90 kilograms).

Freedom Fact!

The first American flag had 13 stars and 13 stripes. The McHenry flag had 15 stars and 15 stripes because two more states, Kentucky and Vermont had been added.

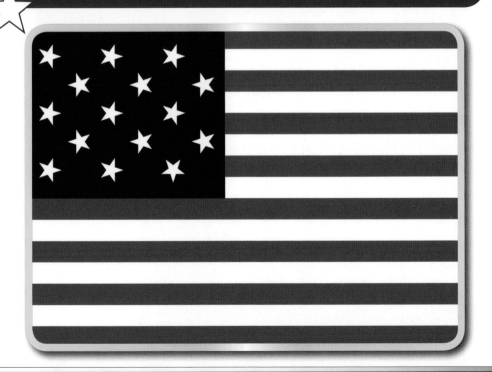

The flag was delivered to Fort McHenry on August 19, 1813 and was soon flying high. Pickersgill's inspirational flag remained at the fort until 1824. When it was taken down, it was given to Major Armistead's family. In 1907, his family donated the huge flag to the Smithsonian Institute's National Museum of American History in Washington, D.C. That famous flag is displayed there today.

Freedom Fact!

Some parts of the Fort McHenry flag are missing. Pieces of the flag were cut away and given to soldiers or the wives of soldiers who served at Fort McHenry. Today, the flag measures 30 feet (9 meters) high and 34 feet (10.4 meters) wide.

The Smithsonian protects and preserves the Fort McHenry flag on display at the Smithsonian Institution.

OUR NATIONAL ANTHEM

After the battle at Fort McHenry, Francis Scott Key shared his poem with a reporter in Baltimore. It was published in the local newspaper on September 20. Soon after, the poem was set to music. Key decided that it should be sung to the tune of "To Anacreon in Heaven." This was a popular old British song. The song was first performed in Baltimore on October 19, 1814.

Key's song inspired American patriotism. It grew more and more popular. People began singing it all over the country. During the Civil War, both Northern and Southern troops sang the song. The army and navy began playing it during important ceremonies. More than 100 years later, Key's poem became the most important song in the country. On March 3, 1931, President Herbert Hoover signed a law making "The Star-Spangled Banner" America's national anthem.

The Star-Spangled Banner

The words of "The Star Spangled Banner" were written by Mr. Key in 1814 under stirring circumstances. He
Was detained on board one of the British ships which attacked Fort McHenry. All night the bombardment continued,
indicating that the fort had not surrendered. Toward the morning the firing ceased, and Mr. Key awaited dawn in great
suspense. When light came, he saw that "our flag was still there," and in the fervor of the moment he wrote the lines of
our national song. the tune is ascribed by the weight of authority to John Stafford Smith, an English composer who set
it about 1780.

Francis Scott Key

John Stafford Smith

Oh,— say, can you see, by the dawn's ear-ly light, What so proud-ly we hailed at the twi-light's last

gleam-ing? Whose broad stripes and bright stars, thro' the per-il-ous fight, O'er the ram-parts we watched were so gal-ant-ly

stream-ing? And the rock-ets' red glare, the bombs burst-ing in air, Gave proof thro' the night that our flag was still

there. Oh, say, does that— star span - gled ban - ner— yet—

wave— O'er the land— of the free and the home of the brave?

2. On the shore, dimly seen thro' the mists of the deep,
Where the foe's haughty host in dread silence reposes,
What is that which the breeze, o'er the towering steep,
As it fitfully blows, half conceals, half discloses?
Now it catches the gleam of the morning's first beam,
In full glory reflected now shines on the stream:
'Tis the star-spangled banner: oh, long may it wave
O'er the land of the free and the home of the brave!

3. Oh, thus be it e'er when free-men shall stand
Between their loved homes and the war's desolation;
Blest with vict'ry and peace, may the heav'n-rescued land
Praise the Pow'r that has made and preserved us a nation!
Then conquer we must, when our cause it is just;
And this be our motto: "In God is our trust!"
And the star-spangled banner in triumph shall wave
O'er the land of the free and the home of the brave!

Freedom Fact!

John Stafford Smith, an English composer, composed the music used for "The Star-Spangled Banner."

The national anthem is an important American tradition. It is performed during official events for our nation, like when the president of the United States takes office. American military forces play the song to honor American soldiers. It is played to celebrate national holidays and special events.

In America, sporting events bring thousands of people together in one place. "The Star-Spangled Banner" starts the event. At the Olympic Games, the national anthem is played when an American athlete wins a medal.

When the American flag flies and the national anthem is played, it unites Americans. It inspires a sense of community and American spirit. Just as the vision of the flag flying over Fort McHenry inspired Francis Scott Key, we are inspired each time we hear his words and music. It renews our sense of pride as citizens of the United States of America.

When the national anthem is played, many Americans feel pride and patriotism.

TIMELINE

1777 —— *First official U.S. flag is adopted with thirteen stars and thirteen stripes.*

1783 —— *U.S. wins the Revolutionary War.*

1795 —— *U.S. Flag is changed to fifteen stars and fifteen stripes.*

1812 —— *On June 18, President James Madison asks Congress to declare war on Britain.*

1813 —— *Fort McHenry receives its new flag on August 19.*

1814 —— *British soldiers invade and burn Washington, D.C. in August.*

Oh,_ say, can you see, by the dawn's ear-ly light, What so proud-ly we hailed at the twi-light's last

1814 —— *On September 10, Francis Scott Key boards a British warship hoping to gain the release of an American prisoner.*

FRANCIS SCOTT KEY.

1814 —— *Americans defend Fort McHenry in a battle against Britain from September 12–14.*

1814 —— *Francis Scott Key writes a poem titled "The Defense of Fort McHenry" on September 14.*

1814 —— *Key's poem, "The Defense of Fort McHenry," is published on September 17.*

1814 —— *In October, "The Star-Spangled Banner" is performed to the tune of "To Anacreon in Heaven."*

1814 —— *The War of 1812 ends in December.*

1931 —— *"The Star-Spangled Banner" is adopted as the U.S. national anthem on March 3.*

gleam-ing? Whose broad stripes and bright stars, thro' the per-il-ous fight, O'er the ram-parts we watched were so gal-ant-ly

GLOSSARY

anthem (AN-thum): a religious or national song

commissioned (kuh-MISH-uhnd): to give someone the power to do something

interfering (in-tur-FIHR-ing): to hinder

mortar (MOR-tur): a very short cannon that fires shells or rockets high in the air

patriotism (PAY-tree-uh-tiz-uhm): showing strong love and support for your country

peninsula (puh-NIN-suh-luh): a piece of land that sticks out from a larger land mass and is surrounded by water on three sides

prosperous (PROSS-pur-uhs): something that is successful or thriving

ransacked (RAN-sakt): searched wildly usually looking for things to steal

relentless (ri-LENT-liss): endless and determined

sloop (SLOOP): a sailboat with one mast and sails that are set from front to back

troops (TROOPS): an organized group of soldiers

INDEX

SHOW WHAT YOU KNOW

1. Explain how and why Fort McHenry played a critical role in the war.

2. What events led up to the War of 1812?

3. Explain the role of "The Star-Spangled Banner" in American culture.

4. Why did the British want to capture Baltimore and what stood in their way?

5. Explain the connection between Francis Scott Key and the Fort McHenry flag.

WEBSITES TO VISIT

www.americaslibrary.gov/index.html

amhistory.si.edu/starspangledbanner

www.nps.gov/fomc/index.htm

ABOUT THE AUTHOR

Cristie Reed loves to travel through the United States and learn about the history of our country. She also likes to learn about the great stories of America through reading and research. She has been a teacher and reading specialist for many years. She lives in central Florida with her husband and pet dog, Rocky.

Meet The Author!
www.meetREMauthors.com

www.rourkeeducationalmedia.com

PHOTO CREDITS: Cover/Title page © LOC; page 4 © charnsitr; page 5 © Chris Minor; page 6, 8, 9, 10, 11, 19, 2, 23 © Wikipedia; page 7, 11, 14, 15, 20 © LOC; page 12 © Visions of America LLC; page 13 © Coast-to-Coast; page 16 © Vasiliki Varvaki; page 17 © PICSUNV; page 24 © Alex Wong; page 26 © John Moore; page 27 © Joe Raedle

Edited by: Jill Sherman

Cover design by: Nicola Stratford, nicolastratford.com
Interior design by: Rhea Magaro

Library of Congress PCN Data

The Star Spangled Banner / Cristie Reed
(Symbols of Freedom)
ISBN 978-1-62717-737-5 (hard cover)
ISBN 978-1-62717-859-4 (soft cover)
ISBN 978-1-62717-970-6 (e-Book)
Library of Congress Control Number: 2014935662

Printed in the United States of America, North Mankato, Minnesota

Also Available as: